Book 4

Strange but true stories

- **What lurks beneath the waves?**
- **Winchester mystery house**
- **Skulls of doom**

... and more!

BY
Janet Lorimer

Strange (but true) stories

BOOK 1

The presidential ghost
Mystery spots on Earth
UFO or weather balloon?

BOOK 2

Bob Lazar, the UFO guy
The Mothman mystery
Mischievous spirits

BOOK 3

The Jersey devil
Phantom ships
Living dinosaurs?

BOOK 4

What lurks beneath the waves?
Winchester mystery house
Skulls of doom

BOOK 5

King Tut's curse
Amazing athletic feats
Monster or myth?

AND MUCH MORE!

First published SADDLEBACK PUBLISHING, INC.
Three Watson Irvine, CA 92618-2767

Published under licence 2007 by R.I.C. PUBLICATIONS® PTY LTD
PO Box 332 Greenwood 6924 Western Australia
www.ricgroup.com.au

Distributed by:
Australasia
R.I.C. Publications, PO Box 332, Greenwood 6924, Western Australia:
www.ricgroup.com.au
United Kingdom and Republic of Ireland
Prim-Ed Publishing, Bosheen, New Ross, Co. Wexford, Ireland:
www.prim-ed.com
Asia
R.I.C. Publications, 5th Floor, Gotanda Mikado Building,
2-5-8 Hiratsuka, Shinagawa-Ku Tokyo, Japan 142-0051:
www.ricpublications.com

ISBN 978-1-74126-651-1

CONTENTS

4

THE MYSTERY OF THE LOST DUTCHMAN MINE

Superstition Mountain is located east of the city of Phoenix in Arizona, USA. It is actually more than one mountain. In fact, it's almost 627 square kilometres of rough terrain. It is here that the famous Lost Dutchman mine is said to be located.

But beware! Many people who have come to this rough region to hunt gold have never been seen again!

When the Spanish first arrived here in 1540, they were looking for gold. The local natives assured them that the mountain held much gold. But then they added that the Thunder God lived on the mountain. He would destroy anyone who trespassed on his sacred ground.

Sure enough, when the Spanish tried to explore the mountain, some of them vanished mysteriously— and the bodies of the men who were found had their heads cut off! The terrified survivors refused to go back to the mountain.

Three centuries passed.

In 1845, Miguel Peralta, a member of a well-to-do family in Sonora, Mexico, actually found the gold. Peralta returned to Mexico to gather people and supplies so he could set up a mining operation.

This angered the Apaches. In 1848, they decided to drive Peralta and his men from the area. Peralta learned of the coming attack. First, he hid the entrance to the mine. Then he and his men loaded up the pack mules with as much gold ore as they could carry.

Sadly, they were too slow. The Apaches attacked, driving the men and the animals over cliffs and into ravines! For many years after, gold hunters found the remains of burros and leather packs still brimming with gold. But none of them could ever find the mine itself.

The next person to find gold in Superstition Mountain was Dr Abraham Thorne. In 1865, he travelled to Arizona to live and work among the natives. He made many friends as he cared for the sick and injured.

After five years, the natives came to him with a proposal. To thank him for his good deeds, they wanted to show where he could find gold. He would have to agree, however, to let them blindfold him on the 32 kilometre journey.

Dr Thorne agreed. When the blindfold was removed, he saw a heap of gold nuggets piled against the canyon wall. It almost looked as if it had been put there for him. He picked up as much as he could carry with him. But he never returned to search for the mine.

Next came the 'Dutchman', Jacob Waltz, who was actually German. He was already a grizzled old prospector when he arrived in Arizona to hunt for gold. There he met Jacob Weiser, and the two men teamed up, hoping to strike it rich.

No-one knows for sure where they got their map to the mine. Some say it was in return for saving the life of Miguel Peralta. He was a descendant of the man who'd first discovered the mine.

At some point after that Jacob Weiser disappeared. Did the natives kill him? Or did his partner, Jacob Waltz, do him in?

Waltz would leave Phoenix for long periods of time. When he returned, he'd be carrying a bag of rich gold ore. He never told anyone where he found the gold and he always managed to get away from anyone who tried to follow him.

In 1891, a Mexican widow named Julia Thomas befriended Waltz. He promised to show her the secret mine, but then he suddenly died. Under his bed was a sack of rich gold ore.

More prospectors began searching for the mine. Dozens of fake maps, books and pamphlets—all supposedly giving the location of the lost mine— were produced.

Many people lost money buying these fake guides—others even lost their lives.

Some men were killed by natives or died in accidents on the mountain.

Other deaths are more mysterious. A few of the prospectors seemed to have simply disappeared— just as the Spanish explorers did in 1540.

Some victims were skeletons when they were found. Some had their heads cut off, while others had bullet holes in their skulls.

Is Superstition Mountain haunted? Are the ghosts of murdered gold hunters protecting the Lost Dutchman mine?

Perhaps the Apaches had it right all along. If the mountain does belong to the Thunder God, it seems he will destroy anyone who trespasses!

Strange but true stories

WHO WAS JACK THE RIPPER?

London, England. 31 August 1888. Mary Ann Nichols was brutally murdered in Whitechapel, an area of terrible poverty in the city's East End.

Eight days later, Annie Chapman's mutilated body was discovered in the same area. Twenty-two days after that, two more women—Elizabeth Stride and Catherine Eddowes—fell victim to the killer.

By now, the people of London—especially in Whitechapel—were in an uproar. Two days before Stride and Eddowes were murdered, the police had received a letter from the killer. It was signed, 'Jack the Ripper'.

Each killing was more hideous than the last. The killer slashed his victims and then removed the body parts! In between killings, Jack the Ripper sent taunting letters to the police.

The police were desperate to find the killer. Of course, they didn't have today's technology to help them, so it wasn't easy. To make matters even worse, evidence was sometimes badly handled.

They did, however, identify some 30 suspects. These included—among others—a surgeon, an artist, a royal physician and even Queen Victoria's grandson!

London's Metropolitan Police finally narrowed down their list to four:

- Aaron Kosminski, a poor resident of Whitechapel. Three years later he was transferred to a mental hospital.

- John Druitt Montague, a lawyer and schoolteacher who drowned in December 1888.

- Dr Francis J Tumblety, an American con artist who was arrested but fled from England after he posted bail.

- Michael Ostrog, a known thief and con man who'd been detained in mental hospitals several times.

Unfortunately, there wasn't enough evidence to hold any of these four men.

The serial killer was credited with one more victim—Mary Jane Kelly—who was murdered on 9 November 1888.

And then the killings stopped.

Or did they?

Many people believe that later killings can be credited to Jack the Ripper. These deaths took place outside of London and in France. Did the Ripper move out of Whitechapel when things got too hot for him?

It's been more than a century since Jack the Ripper stalked the dark streets of Whitechapel. In that time, books, plays, movies, television programs and even a musical have been written about him. There are almost as many theories as there are suspects!

It's likely that we'll never know Jack the Ripper's true identity. Perhaps that's the way some people— possibly even a few of royal descent—want it to be!

Strange *but true* stories

THE SALEM WITCH-HUNT

In today's courts of law, people are considered innocent until proven guilty. About 300 years ago it was the other way around. If you were accused of a crime, you were *guilty* until proven innocent!

January 1692. Salem, Massachusetts. During that cold, dark winter a group of eight girls—ages 9 to 17—began to act very strangely. Some of them had violent seizures. At times their speech was garbled and they seemed to go into a trance-like state. At other times they complained about a crawly feeling on their skin.

No doctor could figure out what was causing the girls to act this way. Finally, the worried parents concluded that the girls were bewitched. They suspected someone in the community must be responsible. It wasn't long before the girls themselves began to point the finger of blame.

1 March: Three women were arrested. The first person the girls had accused of witchcraft was a Caribbean-Indian slave named Tituba. She admitted that she told fortunes. Next, the girls accused Sarah Osborne, an elderly woman that

no-one liked, and Sarah Good, the town beggar. They even accused Sarah Good's four-year-old daughter of being a witch! All the accused were arrested.

As the accusations and arrests continued, the jails were soon filled to capacity. New prisoners had to be sent to jails in nearby communities.

Those accused of witchcraft were first given a physical examination. Why? To see if they had strange marks on their bodies. An odd-looking mole might be the mark of a witch! Then they were questioned. Before the trial they were told to plead guilty. Then, if they named other people as witches, they would be spared. If they didn't, they'd be put to death. Since most refused to plead guilty, they were put on trial.

On 10 June Bridget Bishop—the first person pronounced guilty of witchcraft—was hanged. Before summer ended, 18 more people were hanged.

One elderly man was accused of witchcraft. When he refused to say whether he was innocent or guilty, he was tortured. For three days stones were piled upon him—until the poor old fellow was crushed to death.

At least five—and perhaps as many as 17—more people died in jail. In all, several hundred people were accused of witchcraft and more than 140 went to jail.

Before long, the terror spread—like a disease—to other towns. In July, in the neighbouring town of Andover, the wife of Joseph Ballard became ill. The doctor was at a loss to explain her illness. Ballard became convinced that his wife had been bewitched. He rode to Salem for help. He asked the accusing teenagers to help him find the witches in Andover.

Having become local celebrities, the girls were happy to help. A witch-hunt was soon under way in Andover. The hysteria quickly spread to other towns, including the city of Boston.

In October, people finally began to realise that hysteria and hearsay were fueling the trials. But it wasn't until January 1693 that the trials ended.

Why had it happened? Today, it's hard for us to even imagine a witch-hunt. As it turns out, there may have been more than one reason.

Consider the first two girls to exhibit signs of being bewitched. They were the daughter and niece of Reverend Samuel Parris, a stern Puritan. In fact, *most* of the people who lived around Salem were members of this very strict religious sect. Adults frowned upon playtime for children.

So it's possible that the girls' strange behaviour grew out of boredom and repression.

Rev. Parris strongly supported the witch-hunt. He gave passionate sermons on the subject of witchcraft. The terrified Puritans blamed witches for everything from Native American attacks to spoiled milk! Some survivors of the attacks had taken refuge in Salem. The horrible tales they brought with them fueled everyone's fears. With boredom added to fear, the nervous Puritans were ripe for an attack of mass hysteria.

Another cause could have been the place itself. In 1692, Salem was divided into two areas—Salem Village and Salem Town. The people who lived in Salem Village were mostly poor farmers. The people of Salem Town were mostly carpenters, blacksmiths and innkeepers. They had more money and enjoyed a better life than the struggling farmers. There was some jealousy between the two groups.

A number of prosperous people were accused of witchcraft. In those days, just to be accused was to lose whatever you owned. The local sheriff took possession of your belongings and neighbours took possession of your lands.

Most of the accused were women. Many men believed that women, being inferior to men, were easily turned into witches. Many of the women who were accused were in a position to inherit property. Others were too old or too poor to defend themselves. These factors made women prime targets. Thirteen of the 19 people hanged were women.

Some of the girls' hysterical behaviour was probably faked. During one of the trials, a girl recanted the accusations she had made. Perhaps she was feeling guilty about what was happening in the community. But as a result, the other girls turned on her—and she herself was accused of witchcraft!

There may have been one more reason: Ergot poisoning! Ergot is a fungus that affects grains such as rye and wheat. Rye was a staple grain in Salem. Ergot thrives in the warm, rainy days of spring and summer. Those conditions were present the summer before the witchcraft hysteria broke out. If the grain was infected by ergot, anyone who ate bread made with ergot-infected flour could have had delusions. Other symptoms of ergot poisoning include convulsions, hallucinations and crawling sensations on the skin.

No doubt the hysteria behind the witch-hunts came from several different sources. We may never really know. But we do know how it changed our history.

In October 1692, one clergyman wrote the following: 'It were better that ten suspected witches should escape than that the innocent person should be condemned'. This has evolved into today's 'innocent-until-proven-guilty' justice system. In this way, the terrible events of the witch-hunt had an indirect impact on the founding principles of most governments.

Some 300 years later in Salem, a memorial was erected to honour victims of the witchcraft trials. It is located across the street from the original Salem Village Meeting House. That was where people were examined to see if they were witches.

The memorial now serves as a reminder: We must always be on guard against intolerance, bigotry, prejudice and fanaticism—all of which can fuel 'witch-hunts' of one kind or another.

Strange but true stories

THE SUPERVOLCANO
IN OUR OWN BACKYARD

Yellowstone National Park, located in the United States, is a place of natural wonders, such as Old Faithful, the famous geyser. But most people don't realise that the Park sits on a *caldera*. This is a huge depression created when a volcano erupts. Also, the volcano on this caldera isn't a dead one—it's alive!

Scientists know that in the past this volcano has erupted about once every 600 000 years. The last time it happened was 640 000 years ago. Some scientists believe the next 'big blow' is long overdue!

Most importantly, the volcano under Yellowstone isn't just any old volcano. It's a *supervolcano*!

In all the world, there are only a few supervolcanoes. The last one erupted 74 000 years ago. That eruption was so powerful that it affected all life on Earth! So much ash and sulphur dioxide blasted into the atmosphere that sunlight was blocked. The temperature of the Earth dropped and nothing could grow. The result was mass starvation.

If a supervolcano should erupt today, it would be unlike anything we've ever seen. The explosion would be so loud it would be heard all around the world.

But do we know for certain that the volcano under Yellowstone is ever going to erupt?

The caldera is 48 kilometres wide and 72 kilometres long. In the 1970s, a scientist discovered that the caldera's center had risen nearly one metre since the 1920s. It kept rising until 1985, when several earthquakes rocked the park. Scientists guessed that might mean the gases were escaping. Then the caldera began to deflate—like a balloon!

In 1995, part of the caldera began to inflate again. It stopped in 2002. At the same time scientists discovered a 40 kilometre wide swelling *outside* the caldera near Norris Basin.

In March 2003, fourteen new steam vents opened up. In July 2004, geysers began erupting at strange times. The temperature of the ground shot up. Park rangers had to close off sections of the park until things calmed down.

Most scientists believe that we will know if a huge eruption is coming. There will be signs for weeks, months or even years in advance.

They also believe that the activity noted in geysers, steam vents and earthquakes is normal for the area. They point out that for the past 10 000 years there have been many earthquakes and steam explosions in Yellowstone. None of them has led to a volcanic eruption.

Strange **but true** stories

'CHICKEN SKIN' STORIES FROM HAWAII

In Hawaii, scary stories that give you goose bumps—like ghost stories—are called 'chicken skin' stories.

THE MARCHERS OF THE NIGHT

Some Hawaiians have seen them. And of those who saw them, some even lived to tell the tale!

The Marchers of the Night are ghosts that march together in a procession. They are said to be the spirits of dead chiefs and warriors.

Usually, these marchers are seen at night. Even if you can't see them, you may be able to hear them. They're accompanied by chanting and by music played on the nose flute and drums.

Torches light the procession. At the head of the column of marchers is a ghost carrying a spear. He calls out to warn the living to get out of the way.

'*O`io!*' he cries. 'Run from the spear.'

It's his duty to put to death any living being that's unlucky enough to be standing in the path of the Marchers. Immediate death will come from that ghostly spear.

But what if the human has a family member who's marching in the eerie procession? Recognising the person, the relative's spirit will command the spearman to stop. '*Alia!*'

Then the spearman will refrain from throwing his spear into the human's heart.

The tale is told of a deaf old Japanese man who was night fishing. People who lived near the beach heard the Night Marchers coming and ran off. However, the old man heard nothing. By the time he saw the ghostly procession it was too late! The next morning, people found his body near the water.

The coroner said the old man died of a heart attack, but . . .

How can you save yourself? If you do meet a procession of Night Marchers, you should turn and run. Don't cry out or look back. Don't call attention to yourself.

If you can't get away, then take off all your clothes and throw yourself on the ground, face down. Close your eyes, don't move and don't look up.

Just hope that you don't get a spear thrust through your back!

PELE

Pele is the goddess of the volcano. Most people think of her as a character in an ancient Hawaiian legend.

It never occurs to people that they might encounter her today. But many people say they've seen Pele. Sometimes she appears as an old woman. Sometimes she appears as a young girl.

In 1960, Betty—a radio announcer—went out to dinner with two friends. They headed for Volcano House Hotel on Hawaii's largest island. As they waited for a table, Betty suddenly felt something jab the back of her neck. She turned and saw an elderly Hawaiian woman in a long white dress.

The old woman asked Betty if she was the radio announcer. Betty said she was.

'Within 30 days the island will be visited by Pele', the old woman said. 'The results will be disastrous.'

Then the old woman left. Betty realised that no-one in the crowded restaurant seemed to notice her.

'Well, how about that!' Betty said, turning back to her friends.

'How about what?' one asked.

'That Hawaiian lady I was talking to', Betty said.

Betty's friends looked puzzled. They'd seen Betty turn away, but they hadn't seen a Hawaiian woman—and they hadn't heard any conversation.

Betty was alarmed. She decided she needed to pass on the old woman's warning. So every day for five days, she repeated the warning over and over on the radio.

Exactly 28 days after her meeting with the Hawaiian woman, a tsunami hit Hawaii. Starting with an earthquake off the coast of Chile, the tsunami travelled with such speed that it reached Hawaii in just 15 hours. In the city of Hilo, 61 people were killed!

Had the warning come from Pele herself? Even Betty can't be certain.

Strange but true stories

THE MADMAN
AND THE DICTIONARY

Professor James Murray was quite annoyed. He'd invited Dr William Minor to visit him many times. Why did the man always turn him down?

In 1889, Murray was compiling the first *Oxford English dictionary*. It was a huge, time-consuming job. Nine years before, Murray had advertised for volunteers. He asked people to provide quotations and examples to be used in dictionary definitions.

Dr Minor had responded by mail to the ad—and his help turned out to be priceless! Over several years, he'd mailed in hundreds of neat, well-written quotes and examples.

Dr Minor's letters all came from Broadmoor, a hospital for the criminally insane. Murray figured that he was a busy member of the hospital's staff. But Broadmoor was only 80 kilometres from Oxford! Surely the doctor could take just one day off to come for a visit.

His thoughts were interrupted by a visit from another friend, Dr Winsor, the librarian of Harvard

College. During their pleasant conversation, a chance remark stunned James Murray.

'You've given great pleasure to us Americans', Dr Winsor said. 'We appreciate your speaking so kindly about poor Dr Minor—'

Murray frowned. '*Poor* Dr Minor? What can you possibly mean?'

It was then Murray learned why his invitations had been refused. Dr Minor—one of the greatest contributors to the *Oxford English dictionary*—was in fact a madman!

* * *

William Chester Minor, a surgeon, had joined the Union Army in 1863—at the height of the American Civil War. Did the horrors he witnessed during the war cause his decline into madness? We don't know. By 1868, he was showing symptoms of mental illness and he retired from the army.

In 1872, Dr Minor traveled to London, perhaps to seek a cure. But one night he was convinced that someone had broken into his room. A few hours later he shot and killed an innocent man in the street.

After being arrested, tried and judged to be insane, he was sent to Broadmoor.

As a wealthy man, he had special privileges there. He collected hundreds of books, many of them rare and out-of-print volumes. In 1880, he answered Murray's plea for volunteers.

Murray and Minor finally met at Broadmoor in 1891. Minor's mental illness was obvious. He complained that people broke into his rooms. They assaulted him, he said, and went through his belongings. Murray decided to ignore Minor's paranoia. Instead, the two men talked about shared interests—books, words and the dictionary.

For years, Minor's stepbrother had tried to get Minor returned to America. Finally, in 1910, Minor was released from Broadmoor and returned to the United States.

In 1915, James Murray died. In 1920, Minor also passed away.

As for the *Oxford English dictionary*, it was finally completed in 1927. The enormous project had taken 70 years to complete! It contained definitions for 414 825 words.

Sadly, neither James Murray nor William Minor lived long enough to see the dictionary published.

Strange but true stories

IS AN AFRICAN TRIBE CONNECTED TO A DISTANT STAR?

The Dogon are a tribe of native people living in Africa. Scientists think they may be descended from the ancient Egyptians. A long time ago, they lived in Libya, but some time later they settled in West Africa, where they live today.

For centuries the Dogon were cut off from the outside world. So how could they know so much about a faraway star called Sirius?

In 1931, two French scientists made contact with the Dogon. One of them, Dr Griaule, lived with the tribe for 16 years. Over the years, the village elders came to respect and trust him. In 1947, they shared some of their tribe's secret knowledge with him. None of this information was in writing. All of it had been passed down by word of mouth from one generation to the next.

The Dogon, Griaule discovered, have always had a great interest in studying the heavens. Amazingly, they knew that the moon is dry and barren. They knew about Saturn's rings and that Jupiter has four large moons. They knew that the Milky Way is a spiral galaxy of stars and that planets move around the Sun.

The Dogon have a special respect for the star Sirius. They told Griaule that Sirius is not one star, but three! Griaule was astonished. At that time, scientists knew about a second star, but not a third.

Now we know that the largest and brightest star is Sirius A. Sirius B is a tiny dense star—too small to be seen without a telescope—that travels around Sirius A. Sirius B was first seen in 1862. But it wasn't photographed until 1970.

The Dogon elders claimed that Sirius B is white and very heavy. They said its journey around Sirius A takes about 50 years. In 1926, scientists discovered stars called 'white dwarves'. These are so dense that 1 cubic metre of star matter may weigh up to 20 000 tonnes! Sirius B was exactly what the Dogon had described!

As for the third star in the Sirius system, the Dogon claimed that it also traveled around Sirius A. This third star, according to the Dogon, is much lighter and has a larger orbit than Sirius B. It even has a planet of its own.

The Dogon showed Griaule 400-year-old masks with drawings of these stars and the planet.

They said they used these masks during a special ceremony held once every 60 years. The ceremony represents the renewal of the universe.

How do the Dogon know so much about the universe—especially Sirius B?

They told Griaule that visitors from another world told them about it centuries ago. They call these aliens the *Nommos*. According to the Dogon, the alien creatures were part fish, part human, who spent much of their time in water. Strangely, similar creatures appear in the stories of several other ancient civilizations. The ancient Babylonians, Sumerians and Egyptians had stories of creatures like mermaids and mermen who lived mostly in the sea.

The Nommos told the Dogon they'd traveled to our world from the small planet that orbits Sirius C. They also claimed that someday they would return and rule our world from the water.

As you can imagine, not everyone believes the Dogon's story.

Critics think that the Dogon learned of the stars and planets from missionaries and explorers who visited them. But one writer learned that no missionaries had visited the Dogon before 1949—two years *after* the Dogon shared their secrets with Dr Griaule.

Is an African tribe connected to a distance star?

Critics also claim that no-one has ever carbon-dated the Dogon's old masks. Therefore, we have only the tribe's word that the masks are more than 400 years old.

But what about Sirius C? Is there a third star in the Sirius system? That would certainly help prove that what the Dogon say is true.

Unfortunately, no-one has discovered a third Sirius star. Yet . . .

In 1995, two French astronomers noted a certain turbulence in the Sirius system. They suggested it could be explained by *a third star*!

If scientists do discover that third star, it will go a long way toward proving the Dogon's claim. Then we may indeed have to believe that their knowledge about the stars came *from the stars*!

Strange *but true* stories

CAN DOGS REALLY SMELL CANCER?

The woman was puzzled. Her dog had been acting very strangely. Why did the dog keep sniffing at a mole on her leg? It ignored all the other moles on the woman's body. But the mole on her leg seemed to bother the animal a lot.

Then one day, when the woman was wearing shorts, this gentle dog tried to bite the mole off!

That was enough to send the woman to her doctor. She wanted to have the mole removed. After removing it, the doctor sent it to a lab to be tested. The lab test showed that the mole was a deadly form of skin cancer. Thanks to her dog, the woman's life had been saved!

That happened in 1989 in England. It was the first time anyone had ever imagined that dogs might be able to detect cancer in its early stages.

Dogs *do* have incredible noses. A dog's sense of smell, in fact, is 100 000 times better than a human's!

In England and the United States, dogs are now being trained to sniff out cancers of many types. Prostate cancer, lung cancer and breast cancer have all been 'sniffed out' by trained dogs. Also, many dog breeds show a remarkable talent for the work.

Trainers say that dogs are trained to detect cancer in the same way they're trained to sniff out bombs. The dogs sniff samples of human urine. People with cancer get rid of abnormal cells through their urine. Some samples are from cancer patients, others are not. The dogs have to be trained to tell the difference.

But what are the odds of a dog getting it right?

Amazingly, when trained dogs are tested, they accurately select the cancer samples at least 41 percent of the time. If they were selecting only by chance, the odds are they would be right only 14 percent of the time.

Some dogs are better at detecting cancers than others. Take George, for example. He was especially trained to sniff out melanoma. He correctly smelled this deadly skin cancer 99 percent of the time!

Of course, cancer-sniffing dogs have their critics. Some scientists say that it's silly to think that dogs can sniff out cancer. One scientist claims that other human body odours are simply too strong. They say the smells would cover up the odour of cancer cells.

But one veterinarian points out that cancer affects a person's metabolism. This vet believes that what dogs are detecting is this change in metabolism.

Doctors who believe that dogs can detect cancer like to tell the following story. Six dogs were being trained to detect cancer cells in urine. Some of the samples came from cancer patients. Some did not. But, oddly, all six dogs identified one sample as containing cancer cells.

The trainers couldn't figure that one out. The urine samples had all been carefully screened. But the screening showed no trace of cancer in this particular person.

After conducting more tests on that patient, doctors found a life-threatening tumour in the person's right kidney!

The dogs had found the cancer before the doctors. Once again, their early detection saved that person's life!

Strange but true stories

THE WOMAN SPY WHO SAVED GEORGE WASHINGTON

There are many well-known heroes of the American Revolution, America's war of independence against Britain. George Washington, Thomas Jefferson, Benjamin Franklin, to name just a few.

What about Lydia Darragh? Her name isn't familiar—but this quiet woman was indeed a great heroine of the American Revolution.

Lydia Darragh, her husband and their children lived in Philadelphia. In 1777, when British troops took over the city, Major John Andre ordered the Darraghs to move out of their house. British officers wanted to use their home's big parlour as a meeting room.

Lydia begged the soldiers not to evict her family. They had nowhere else to go. Finally, the British agreed that the Darraghs could stay—on one condition. The British soldiers must be allowed to use the parlour whenever they needed to. Lydia quickly agreed.

On 2 December, Major Andre told her they would need the parlour that night. He warned Lydia that she and every member of her family had to be in bed by 8.00 pm. The family did as they were told, but Lydia could not sleep. She had a feeling that something important was being planned. Lately, she'd noticed that British troops had been drilling more than ever. What were they up to?

At last her curiosity got the better of her. Lydia crept out of bed, tiptoed down the stairs and listened at the parlour door. What she heard was startling. General George Washington and his men were camped at a place called White Marsh. The British were planning an attack on American troops there—an attack that could change the outcome of the war!

When the meeting ended, Lydia ran upstairs and climbed into bed just in time. A moment later she heard footsteps.

Lydia didn't sleep much the rest of the night. She knew she had to warn General Washington about the attack. But how? Then, just before dawn, she finally came up with a plan.

At breakfast she told her husband and children that she needed to get flour. As soon as they left the house, Lydia wrote the important information on a small piece of paper. She rolled it up, hid it in her needle case and stuffed the needle case deep inside her pocket.

Lydia couldn't go to a corner store or supermarket for flour. She had to walk eight kilometres to the flour mill in Frankford. But first she had to get a permit, which would allow her to pass through British lines.

Frankford was a small town that was located in a kind of no-man's land, occupied by neither British nor American troops.

The head of the American spy network—General Elias Boudinot—knew the town well. He made the Rising Sun Tavern there his unofficial headquarters. Lydia intended to give her information to Boudinot himself.

When she reached the British sentries, she explained she was going for flour. She showed her pass and an empty flour sack. Luckily, they didn't search her.

Once at the mill, she left the flour sack to be filled and continued on. Suddenly, she spotted an American officer she knew, Lt Colonel Thomas Craig.

He was very surprised to see her. 'What are you doing here?' he asked as he dismounted from his horse.

Lydia knew she could trust him. She told him she had important information for General Washington. Lt Col. Craig was stunned. This was exactly the information Washington and his troops needed! They knew the British were planning an attack—but they had no idea when and where it would happen. They also didn't know how much weaponry the British had.

Craig promised to deliver the information to General Washington. Then he led Lydia to a farmhouse near the mill. He said it would be safe for her to wait there for her flour.

But Lydia paced nervously. What if something happened to Craig? What if he couldn't get to Washington in time? The attack was only two days away.

In the Rising Sun Tavern, Boudinot was sitting with some of his men. They didn't notice the small, plain-faced woman entering the room. She walked to where Boudinot was sitting and said something to him. At the same time she slipped a small, dirty-looking needle case into his hand. Boudinot glanced down at it. When he looked up, the woman was gone. He hadn't even gotten her name.

Boudinot opened the case and began to search through its narrow pockets. In the last pocket, he found a small piece of paper. Written on it was the information Washington needed to prepare for the British attack.

Meanwhile, Lydia Darragh collected her bag of flour and started back to Philadelphia. By the time she arrived home, it was well after dark.

Late that night, after everyone else was in bed, Lydia sat up, listening and wondering. She could hear the roll of drums as the British troops marched out of Philadelphia. Had General Washington received her information? Had there been enough time to prepare for the attack?

Several days went by. Lydia still didn't know what had happened. But then British soldiers started to trail back into the city.

One night she answered a sharp knock on her door. Her heart almost skipped a beat to see Major John Andre! Did he know what she'd done? Had he come to arrest her?

Andre looked angry. He wanted to speak to Lydia alone. She took him to the parlour and waited.

'Mrs Darragh, the night of our last meeting, was your family in bed?'

'Yes', Lydia said. That was not a lie. Everyone else had been in bed.

Major Andre frowned. 'Well, I need not ask about you', he went on. 'I know that you were asleep because I had to knock three times before you heard me.'

Lydia said nothing.

'But one thing is certain', Andre said. 'The enemy knew we were coming. They were well-prepared. I can't imagine who could have told General Washington our plans, unless ...'

Lydia barely dared to breathe as she waited for him to finish.

'... unless the walls of this house could speak.' He glanced around angrily and then went on. 'When we reached White Marsh, they were waiting for us. We were forced to march back to Philadelphia like a parcel of fools!'

Lydia could barely contain her joy! The British had been defeated. In fact, this proved to be a turning point in the war. Nine months after the British took over Philadelphia, they were forced to leave!

Many years later, Lydia's daughter, Ann, told the story of her mother's bravery. Some didn't believe it. After all, George Washington didn't approve of women spies—even though Lydia's information had helped the war effort. To this day no-one can *prove* who gave Elias Boudinot the information Washington needed.

Most people believe it was Lydia Darragh.

Strange but true stories

SOLDIERS WHO REFUSED TO SURRENDER

World War II ended in 1945. For most of the weary soldiers around the world, it was time to go home. They were more than ready to put down their weapons and pick up the pieces of their lives.

But not all soldiers believed that the war was really over.

In 1944, Lt Onada was sent by the Japanese army to a remote island in the Philippines. He and his men were to conduct guerrilla warfare there. 'It may take three years', his commanding officer told him. 'It may take five—but whatever happens, we'll come back for you. Until then, so long as you have one soldier, you are to continue to lead him.'

The young lieutenant took his commander's words to heart!

Once on the island, Onada and his men were supposed to blow up the pier at the harbour. Next, they were ordered to destroy the airfield.

But the Allies overran the island before the Japanese could complete the job.

Splitting into groups of three or four, Onada and his men retreated into the interior of the island. They had very little food, limited ammunition and only the clothes they were wearing.

Time went by. The groups used guerrilla tactics to fight in skirmishes. Many of the soldiers in other groups were killed, but Lt Onada and his three men survived. Their rations were tight. They added coconuts and bananas to their small supply of rice. Once, they killed a civilian's cow for food.

In October 1945, a leaflet claiming the war was over fell from an airplane. But Onada didn't believe it. Certain that it was only propaganda, he and his men continued to hide.

More leaflets were dropped from planes. Newspapers were left for the soldiers to read. Photographs and letters from relatives were dropped. Friends and relatives spoke out over loudspeakers. But Onada and his men were always suspicious, so they remained hidden.

The years went by. The four men huddled together in the rain. They searched for food together. Sometimes they fired on native islanders, believing they were enemy soldiers in disguise.

In 1949, one of the men left the others and surrendered. In 1953, another man was killed in a skirmish on the beach. The two men who remained—Kozuka and Onada—continued to live in the jungles for another 20 years! They believed their job was to hide behind enemy lines to gather information. During all those years, they awaited the day when Japanese troops would return and retake the Philippine islands.

In October 1972, after 27 years in hiding, Kozuka was killed in a clash with a Filipino patrol. Now Onada was on his own.

In 1974, a Japanese college dropout named Norio Suzuki told his friends he was going to travel through the Philippines. He joked that he planned to find Lt Onada. Amazingly, he did!

Suzuki tried to convince Onada that World War II was really over. Onada claimed that he would only surrender if his commander ordered him to.

Suzuki returned to Japan and found the elderly commander, Major Taniguchi. Taniguchi travelled to the Philippines and met with Onada.

When Onada read the orders stating that all combat activity must cease, he was shocked. It took a while for the news to sink in. Then he realised that he had spent 29 years as a guerrilla fighter in a war that no longer existed. That made him very angry.

Lt Onada was not the only Japanese soldier to continue to hide after the war. In 1972, Shoichi Yokoi surrendered on the island of Guam. In 1974, Teruo Nakamura surrendered on Morotai Island in Indonesia.

Perhaps one of the strangest stories concerns what Japanese officials called 'the doomed and living Robinson Crusoes'.

During the war, a group of survivors—from several Japanese ships that had been sunk—made it to the island of Anatahan. They survived by living a primitive life. They built palm frond huts and ate coconuts, taro, wild sugar cane, fish and lizards.

Just before the war ended, an American bomber crashed on the island, killing the entire crew. In their fight to survive, the Japanese soldiers cannibalised the plane. They made crude pots, knives and roofing for their huts from the metal. Nylon parachutes were turned into clothing. Cords from the parachutes became fishing lines. Springs from machine guns were turned into fishhooks.

People from a nearby island discovered the Japanese. The navy dropped pamphlets to inform these holdouts that the war was over. The men ignored the pamphlets.

Eventually, members of their families wrote letters, which were dropped to the holdouts.

Finally, in June 1951, 'Operation Removal' got under way. Only then did the survivors formally surrender.

World War II has been over for 60 years—for most of us. But perhaps not for all of us!

Strange but true stories

APOLLO 11 AND THE UFO

The 1969 flight of *Apollo 11* from Earth to the moon is historic. It was on this mission that humans first set foot on the moon. But were we the first *living beings* to visit the moon? Maybe not.

After the flight of *Apollo 11*, stories of aliens on the moon began to spread. Supposedly, two of the astronauts—Neil Armstrong and Edwin 'Buzz' Aldrin—saw UFOs shortly after they landed on the moon. But according to 'unnamed sources', NASA blocked these reports from the general public.

Just what was it that the astronauts supposedly saw? Unconfirmed reports say they observed spacecraft on the moon. The following is alleged to be an exact transcript of a radio transmission between *Apollo 11* and NASA:

NASA: What's there?

Apollo 11: These 'babies' are huge, sir. Enormous. Oh, my god! You wouldn't believe it. I'm telling you there are other spacecraft out there. Lined up on the far side of the crater edge. They're on the moon watching us.

Stories about what the astronauts had seen continued to spread. Supposedly, alien beings had a moon base known as Luna. It was said that the aliens had a huge mining operation on the far side of the moon. Their mother ships were also kept there. Smaller flying saucers were sent from Luna to Earth.

This was why, the unnamed sources claimed, Americans couldn't build a base of their own on the moon.

Supposedly, Neil Armstrong told a professor at a NASA conference: 'The fact is, we were warned off by the aliens. There was never any question then of a space station or a moon city'.

When the professor asked for details, Armstrong is said to have added, 'I can't go into details. Let me just say that their ships were far superior to ours, both in size and technology'.

To back up these stories, photographs of UFOs and tapes of the transmissions between NASA and *Apollo 11* were also circulated.

But was any of it true?

In 1980, *Omni* magazine interviewed astronaut Gordon Cooper. He flew on the *Mercury 9* and *Gemini 5* missions.

During the interview, the reporter asked Cooper about the *Apollo 11* mission. Was it true that the astronauts had seen a number of UFOs?

Cooper denied it. He claimed that the tapes and photos had all been faked. He also said that the stories making the rounds were untrue, as well.

But then the reporter asked Cooper about his own experience with UFOs. 'Didn't you go after some UFOs as an Air Force pilot in Germany in the 1950s?'

Cooper agreed that he had. 'Yes, several days in a row we sighted groups of metallic, saucer-shaped vehicles at great altitudes over the base. We tried to get close to them. But they were able to change direction faster than our fighters.'

Cooper went on to say that he did believe in the existence of UFOs. 'I'm sure that at least *some* of the UFOs are not from anywhere on Earth', he added.

He said he believes that people need to know the truth, whatever it may be. 'The more we know', he explained, 'the greater the likelihood of treating UFOs in a friendly fashion'.

Strange but true stories

STRANGE THINGS THAT RAIN DOWN ON US

'It's raining cats and dogs!'

Ever heard that expression? To most of us, that's just another way of saying it's raining heavily.

But what if it really *did* rain cats and dogs? Don't laugh. Those might be the only things that *haven't* rained down on people—so far!

Strange rain is a very weird event and these rains have been documented:

On a quiet street in Southampton, England, the residents lived uneventful lives—until 12 February 1979. That was the day it began to rain seeds—mustard and watercress, to be exact. The next day, down came a shower of peas, corn and beans. Every time one resident opened her front door, masses of bean seeds shot down the hall and into her kitchen!

The third day, a different type of bean seeds fell. In all, 25 'showers' of seeds fell in the neighbourhood. The neighbours collected the seeds and planted them. Everything 'grew beautifully', as they put it. But where had the seeds come from? To this day, no-one knows.

Seeds are among the nicer things to rain from the sky. In 1873, the magazine *Scientific American* reported that frogs had rained down on Kansas City. The city was blanketed with the animals!

In fact, frogs, fish, worms and even slime have rained down on people all around the world.

In July 2001, a strange red rain fell in India. When the rain was analysed, it turned out to be fungus spores. But where had they come from?

One theory is that a freak tornado or whirlwind picks up things, such as fish or frogs. Then the storm carries them for hundreds of kilometres before it dumps them. But that doesn't explain why only certain types of fish are sucked up into the storm. Or why only certain types of seeds are carried off.

Even stranger things have rained down from the skies.

In 1877, several baby alligators—each one about 30 centimetres long—fell on a farm in South Carolina. They landed unharmed. In 1996, a town in Tasmania was 'slimed' with either fish eggs or baby jellyfish.

So that old expression might not be such an exaggeration as it seems. Some day it really *may* rain cats and dogs!

Strange but true stories

WHAT LURKS BENEATH THE WAVES?

In December 1938, a sea captain caught a strange-looking fish off the coast of South Africa. The captain and his crew didn't know what kind of fish it was. So they took it to a local museum.

The museum director contacted an expert on African fish. It turned out that this odd-looking creature was a truly amazing discovery! The fish was a Coelacanth (*SEE-la-kanth*).

Scientists thought that these fish had died out with the dinosaurs—about 80 million years ago. They had no idea that the Coelacanth still existed. All they knew about these fish had been learned from examining fossils.

Then in July 1998, another type of Coelacanth was caught near Indonesia. The existence of these 'living fossils' was a major discovery of the 20th century!

Perhaps other animals that scientists thought were extinct still exist.

* * *

There's another fish that scientists believe is extinct. But is it?

That's a shark called Megalodon, a relative of the great white shark.

Hundreds of this creature's teeth have been brought up from oceans and rock beds. These are fossilised teeth about 10 to 15 centimetres long! That size tooth would make this fish one of the largest that ever lived—possibly as long as 24 metres!

In the 1900s, two Megalodon teeth were brought up from the bottom of the Pacific Ocean. One tooth was only 11 000 years old. That may seem very old to us, but remember that the Coelacanth fish was alive when scientists thought it was long extinct. So what do you think? Could the huge Megalodon shark still be lurking in the ocean depths?

In 1918, some crayfish fishermen in Australia refused to go fishing after a scary encounter at sea. The men claimed that a huge shark had appeared in their fishing grounds. It had taken one crayfish trap after another. Each trap, or 'pot', as they are called, was over one metre in diameter. Each contained two or three dozen crayfish, weighing several kilograms. The shark took the pots, crayfish, mooring lines and all!

The fishermen were familiar with whales—and they all agreed that no whale had done it. They were certain it was a shark and that its colour was ghostly white—the colour of Megalodon.

* * *

In November 1976, a US naval research ship off the coast of Hawaii got a big surprise. The crew accidentally netted a fish that was new to science—a large filter-feeding shark.

The animal was 4.5 metres long and it had seven rows of needle-sharp teeth.

The Hawaiian newspapers ran with the story. They nicknamed the shark 'Megamouth', and the name stuck.

Just nine years later, a second Megamouth shark was netted near Santa Catalina Island off the coast of California.

About two years after that, a five metre Megamouth shark washed up on a beach in Australia. Then, in 1989, two more were recorded in Japan.

Science got a big break in 1990, when fishermen caught a live Megamouth shark. It was carefully towed to shore, where it was studied and photographed. Then it was released back into the ocean with a sonic transmitter attached to it. Scientists have been studying the fish to learn more about its habits.

How many other unknown creatures inhabit the ocean?

Strange but true stories

THE WINCHESTER MYSTERY HOUSE

Many of us believe that our problems would be solved if we were rich. But does money really solve all problems?

It didn't do much to ease the pain of Sarah Winchester—but perhaps it helped in another strange way!

In 1862, Sarah Pardee married William Winchester in Connecticut. William owned a company that developed the repeating rifle. This gun soon became very popular. Sales of the weapon made Winchester a very wealthy man.

Four years after William and Sarah were married, she gave birth to a baby girl. Sadly, their infant daughter died just nine days later.

Sarah was absolutely devastated. She almost lost her mind with grief. It took her nearly ten years to move beyond this tragedy. She never had another child.

Then, in 1881, her husband William died of tuberculosis.

Sarah inherited a huge fortune—more than 20 million dollars. She also inherited nearly half of the Winchester Rifle Company and an income of $1000 a day! This was an incredible amount of money, especially in the late 1800s!

However, the money did nothing to ease Sarah's pain. She continued to grieve deeply for both her husband and her child.

Finally, a friend suggested that Sarah talk to a psychic about her loss, and Sarah agreed. The results were startling. The psychic told Sarah that there was a curse on her family. The curse stemmed from the repeating rifle that William had invented. The spirits of the thousands of people killed by that weapon were now seeking revenge!

The psychic told Sarah that she must sell her home in Connecticut and move west as soon as possible.

'It's time to start a new life', the psychic said. 'Go and build a home for yourself—and for the spirits who have fallen from this terrible weapon. But just remember this: You can *never* stop building the house. If you continue to build, you will live. *Stop and you will die!*'

Sarah did what the psychic told her to do. In 1884, she travelled west until she reached the

Santa Clara Valley in the state of California. There she found a half-finished six-room house on 162 acres. Sarah bought the place and began to build.

Sarah had no master plan for the building. Each morning she met with the foreman and they'd go over her sketched plans for that day's work. She paid local workers to build and rebuild, change, tear down and start building again. For 36 years she kept 22 carpenters working year around—*24 hours a day!*

The house grew to a height of seven storeys. Inside, there were three elevators and 47 fireplaces, staircases that led nowhere and doors that opened onto blank walls. In fact, some doors opened onto steep drops to the lawn outside! All of the stair railings were put in upside down. And for some unknown reason, glass doors were used on many of the bathrooms.

Sarah was fascinated with the number 13. Nearly all the windows had 13 panes of glass. Walls had 13 panels. Some of the rooms had 13 windows. All but one staircase had 13 steps.

That one was a winding staircase with 42 steps. That should have made the staircase three storeys high, but the staircase is only 2.7 metres tall! That's because each stair step is only *five centimetres high*!

All of these strange things seemed to make perfect sense to Sarah. This was her way of controlling the bad spirits she believed were haunting her house. She had deliberately designed her house as a maze to keep the spirits confused.

In 1906, the great San Francisco earthquake rocked the area and damaged part of the Winchester mansion. The top three floors plunged into the gardens and the fireplace in Sarah's room collapsed, trapping the aging widow.

She was rescued, but now she was sure that the spirits were angry. Why? Because she was close to finishing the house. So she decided to board up 30 incomplete rooms, guaranteeing that the construction would never be finished. She'd come to believe that the spirits were trapped inside that section of the house.

Construction began again. Throughout the house, Sarah had a number of chimneys built that served no purpose. Perhaps she believed the old stories about spirits appearing and disappearing through chimneys.

Another odd thing is that only two mirrors were put up in the house. Sarah believed that ghosts were afraid of their own reflections.

On 4 September 1922, Sarah died in her sleep. She was 83 years old.

She left everything to her niece, Frances Marriot, who'd been helping the old woman with her business affairs. By this time, however, Sarah's large fortune had dwindled considerably.

A rumour circulated that a safe with a fortune in it was somewhere in the house. But even though a number of safes were found, all they had inside were old fish lines, socks and other odd items.

Sarah's mansion was sold to a group of investors who planned to use it as a tourist attraction. One of the first visitors was the famous Robert L Ripley. He wrote about the house in his popular newspaper column, 'Believe it or not'.

Today the house is a historical landmark. It now sits on only four acres of land, but it still contains 160 rooms, including 30 bedrooms, five or six kitchens and two ballrooms. The current price tag on the house is at least five and a half million dollars.

As for the spirits, a number of people claim that they still wander around the place. And one of those spirits, it is said, is the ghost of Sarah Winchester!

Strange but true stories

SKULLS OF DOOM

One of the strangest 'gems' in the world is a skull carved from pure quartz crystal. It is said that the eyes are prisms that reveal the future. It has been called the Skull of Doom.

This skull, along with many others, has fascinated researchers for years. Why and how were these skulls made? Where did they come from? How old are they?

According to Native American legend, there are 13 ancient skulls that can speak. It is said that if ever they are brought together, they will predict the future of the world. So far, however, that hasn't happened. Most of the skulls are privately owned. Three of them are in museums.

Some people believe the skulls were put on earth by alien beings or made in the lost city of Atlantis. Many believe the skulls have knowledge of ancient times on Earth as well as of the future.

Some of the skulls are carved from clear quartz. But others have been carved from coloured quartz, making them pink, smoky gray, lavender, red and green.

Most of the skulls were carved in one piece, but two skulls have removable jaws. Some are very small; some are life-sized. Some are quite lightweight, while the heaviest one weighs 18 kilograms!

Many of the skulls have been given nicknames by their owners. There is, of course, the Skull of Doom. But other names are less scary. For example, E.T. is named for its pointed head and overbite. Its owner says it looks like the skull of an alien.

The owners often take their skulls on tour. It is said by some that when any of these skulls are together they seem to communicate with each other. Might the skulls have healing and supernatural powers, as some people have claimed?

One of the skulls is owned by the British Museum. As the story goes, the people who clean the museum each night worry about the skull's gaze. They insist that the skull be covered with a black cloth before they go to work.

How old are these skulls? It's not possible to accurately date stone. So it's been hard to trace the skulls back to the people who made them.

Until recently it was assumed that the skulls were thousands of years old. In 1996, however, the British Broadcasting Corporation in London asked the owners to allow experts to test the skulls. Most of the owners agreed. The results were surprising. At least two of the skulls had tool marks indicating that they'd been carved in the 1800s.

Regardless of their age, these crystal skulls are truly amazing and beautiful gemstones. And no matter what powers they may or may not possess, they leave us with a fascinating sense of mystery.